BRITAIN IN OLD PHOT

AROUND HEATHROW

PAST & PRESENT

PHILIP SHERWOOD

SUTTON PUBLISHING

Sutton Publishing Limited
Phoenix Mill · Thrupp · Stroud
Gloucestershire · GL5 2BU

First published 2006

Copyright © Philip Sherwood, 2006

Title page photograph: Harvest Supper, Sipson
Farm, *c.* 1950 (see page 60).

British Library Cataloguing in Publication Data
A catalogue record for this book is available from the
British Library.

ISBN 0-7509-4135-9

Typeset in 10.5/13.5pt Photina.
Typesetting and origination by
Sutton Publishing Limited.
Printed and bound in England by
J.H. Haynes & Co. Ltd, Sparkford.

*Philip Sherwood is a retired chemist turned local historian who as a Principal
Scientific Officer in the Scientific Civil Service has worked for the Transport (formerly
Road) Research Laboratory and the Royal Commission on Environmental Pollution.
He is an active member of several amenity and environmental groups, the Publications
Editor of the Hayes and Harlington Local History Society and former Chairman of the
local branch of the Campaign for the Protection of Rural England. In addition to
several technical publications he has compiled four previous publications in this series:*
Around Hayes & West Drayton in Old Photographs *(1996);* Around Hayes &
West Drayton: A Second Selection *(1998);* Around Hayes & West Drayton: A
Third Selection *(2002) and* Around Hayes & West Drayton: Transport &
Industry *(2004). In a related series, he is also author of* Heathrow: 2,000 Years of
History *(1999).*

'If you turn down from the Bath Road by the "Three Magpies" you will come across a
road that is as rural as anywhere in England. It is perhaps not scenically wonderful but
for detachment from London or any urban interests it would be hard to find its equal.
There is a calmness and serenity about it that is soothing in a mad rushing world.'

Gordon Maxwell, *Highwayman's Heath*, 1935

'If there was an international prize for the ugliest urban landscape some of the
leading contenders would certainly be around a number of the world's leading
airports. . . . What we finish up with all too frequently is an unappealing wasteland
of warehouses, car parks and poor housing.'

Hudson and Pettifer, *Diamonds in the Sky*, 1979

CONTENTS

British Legion Dinner. The British Legion was founded in 1921 as a voice for the ex-service community and nearly all the men who had served in the forces became members. The Harmondsworth branch of the Legion was very active and arranged many social functions for its members and their families and for the wider community. The picture was taken at the annual Legion dinner for the members held at the Peggy Bedford (see page 36) in the early 1930s. All the men would have been awarded medals and many can be seen wearing them. *(Uxbridge Library)*

ACKNOWLEDGEMENTS

Sincere thanks are due to all the many people who helped in providing information and photographs for inclusion in this book. They include Terry White of the Hayes and Harlington Local History Society, whose vast knowledge provided the material for many of the captions of the photographs of Hayes, Carolynne Cotton and Gwyn Jones of Hillingdon Local Studies, Archives and Museum Service in Uxbridge Library, Josh Hayles, Stan Heyward, Malcolm Heyward, Dave McCartney, the late Josh Marshall, Ken Pearce, the late Peter Philp, Linda Pocklington, Douglas Rust, John Walters and William Wild. The individuals and commercial organisations that provided illustrative material are acknowledged, where appropriate, in the captions to the relevant photographs. Where no acknowledgement is given the illustration is taken from the author's own collection.

The following abbreviations are used in the credits: HHLHS – the Hayes and Harlington Local History Society and WDLHS – the West Drayton and District Local History Society.

Ordnance Survey map of 1935 depicting most of the area covered by the book. The Bath Road (A4) runs east–west across the centre of the map. To the north are the villages of Harlington, Sipson and Harmondsworth, all well away from the main road; to the west is Longford, the only village that is on the Bath Road itself. To the south is the hamlet of Heathrow, straggling along Heathrow Road.

INTRODUCTION

Three previous books in this series under the general title *Around Hayes & West Drayton in Old Photographs* have already appeared. As the title suggests, all these books included photographs of West Drayton and Yiewsley. This time they have been omitted because of the recent publication (2003) of a book of photographs dealing exclusively with these two places. The present book therefore confines itself to Harlington, Harmondsworth, Heathrow, Sipson, Longford and Hayes. This area has been subject to drastic change in the last hundred years; in the 1930s agriculture was still the primary industry but the development of Heathrow Airport dramatically altered the landscape. It is doubtful if any comparable rural area has seen such changes in such a short passage of time. Although the book is not primarily concerned with the airport as such, the 60th anniversary of the inaugural flight from Heathrow will occur in 2006.

The hamlet of Heathrow was obliterated by the airport in 1944 and if the aviation industry has its way the other settlements, with the exception of Hayes, will go the same way. With the threatened destruction of the villages to the north of Heathrow it therefore seems appropriate to consider by means of photographs, both old and new, what has already been lost and what could yet be destroyed in the future by the aviation industry's insatiable demands for continual expansion. If somebody had set out with the declared intention of destroying all evidence of the past they could hardly have done better.

Although the captions in the previous books in the series gave information linking the old photograph to the present, no attempt was made to offer a visual comparison. This is the main aim of the present book, where an earlier photograph appears with one taken recently. Some of the 'old' photographs have appeared in previous publications but all of the modern photographs have been taken in the last ten years, most of them specifically for inclusion in this book.

The book starts with a comparison of old photographs of Heathrow with the present-day airport. So much has been completely obliterated that it is of necessity a brief section as it is almost impossible to link the past with the present. It then proceeds with a journey along the Bath Road from Cranford Bridge to Mad Bridge at Longford. Here too, much has been changed by the close proximity of the airport, but surprisingly much of the old village of Longford still remains. The journey then continues back from Longford via Harmondsworth, Sipson and Harlington, finally ending up in Hayes. This has been included because, like all the other settlements, it is part of the present-day parliamentary constituency of Hayes and Harlington. However, being more remote from the airport, its nature has been changed more by the rapid industrialisation of the town that occurred in the early part of the twentieth century.

P.T. Sherwood
Harlington, 2006

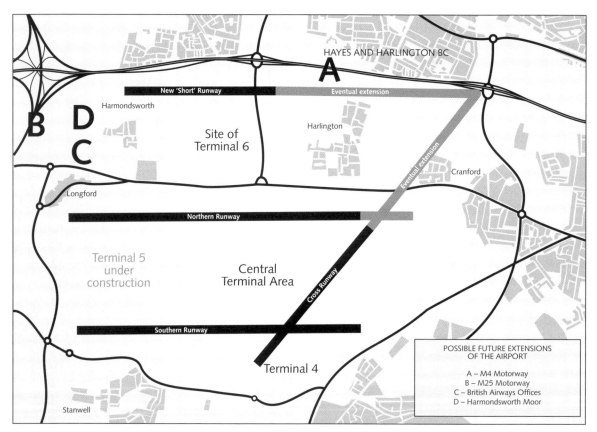

The final solution. In spite of repeated denials, in mid-2005 the British Airports Authority published its master plan for the further development of Heathrow. This envisaged the construction of a 'short' east–west runway between the Bath Road and the M4 motorway, with the construction of a sixth terminal to service the runway. BAA acknowledged that this would involve the destruction of the village of Sipson but assumed that what was left of Longford, Harmondsworth and Harlington could remain as enclaves between the runways. In fact they would be made uninhabitable and there is no denying the fact that the master plan if implemented would lead to the destruction of all three villages. Nor would it end there, as the map shows how easy it would be to lengthen the 'short' runway to make it as long as the other two east–west runways. The existing cross runway could then be linked to the newly lengthened third runway to give Heathrow four main runways. This has been the aim of the aviation industry for the past sixty years. If the plan were to be fully implemented, every scene depicted in this book (with the exception of those of Hayes) would be buried under concrete.

1

Heathrow

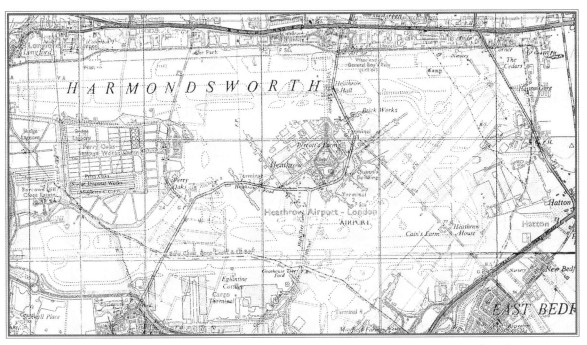

Heathrow, 1935 and 1990. This is the southern section of the 1935 map reproduced on page 4 on which has been superimposed the faint image of a 1990 map at the same scale. It shows how the hamlet of Heathrow was completely obliterated so that it is not possible to depict very many convincing 'before and after' photographs. However, some attempt has been made to do this in the following section, where a comparison of the two maps enables vantage points to be identified.

Ploughing match at Heathrow, 1935. The plough teams are working on what is now part of the northern runway. In the background are some buildings on the Bath Road at Harmondsworth that are still there. (*Uxbridge Library*)

A BOAC Argonaut standing close to the Public Enclosure in the early 1950s. The factory chimney in the background on the right is that of Technicolor Ltd on the Bath Road. The buildings in the background of the previous photograph are obscured by the spectators standing on the left. In the early days of the airport the public were able to view traffic movements at close quarters. Later people could watch from the roof of the Queen's Building but this was closed at the turn of the twenty-first century because of the risk of terrorist attacks. (*P. Donovan*)

The Fairey Aviation Company was founded in 1915 and moved to a site in North Hyde Road, Harlington, in 1917. For a short time it used a field adjacent to its factory there for its trial flights and this photograph shows one of its products. In the left background is the first multi-storey factory building of the Gramophone Company (EMI). The North Hyde Road field proved inadequate for trial flights and the company gained permission from the RAF to use Northolt.

When the RAF revoked the permission to use Northolt in 1929, Fairey Aviation developed its own aerodrome on 200 acres of land in Cains Lane, Heathrow. This photograph shows the airfield in the early 1930s. Fifteen years later the Air Ministry requisitioned the airfield for the development of Heathrow Airport. The loss of its airfield delivered a blow to the company from which it never recovered and it was taken over by Westland Helicopters in 1960. *(B. Cockram)*

Left: The Duke of Northumberland's river at Heathrow, 1921. The river formed the southern boundary of the parish of Harmondsworth and was crossed by a ford in High Tree Lane. The ford was an attractive area popular with courting couples and for picnics, and a riverside path ran from the ford to Longford about 2 miles distant (see below). The river is largely man-made and derives its name from the fact that it was cut in the seventeenth century to supply water to Syon House, the home of the Duke of Northumberland.

Below: The river from Longford Bridge, 2005. The river originally ran from here to Heathrow with a footpath alongside, the beginning of which can be seen on the left of the picture. Until 2003 the river ran due south in a straight line to pass through the Perry Oaks sludge works. In the distance the Terminal 5 building, which will occupy the site of the sludge works, can be seen in the course of construction. This has caused the further diversion of the river so that instead of flowing south, as can be seen it now makes a 90-degree turn to the west.

When development of the airport began in 1944 the Duke of Northumberland's river was diverted to a more southerly course. The construction of Terminal 5 meant that an additional 2 miles of the river had to be diverted westwards, together with a 1½ mile section of the Longford river. The photograph shows the diverted twin rivers to the north of the T5 Welcome Roundabout, Heathrow Airport, on 14 May 2004 soon after the completion of the diversions. The Longford river is on the right, with the Duke of Northumberland's river on the left. Some attempt was made to re-create the appearance of the riverbanks but it contrasts badly with the previous scenes. In any case it has since been completely negated by the need to cover the rivers with netting to deter water birds that might pose a hazard to aircraft. *(D. McCartney)*

Farmland, Hatton Road, 1944. The land in the foreground is still under cultivation but work on the construction of the airport is just about to start and huts are being erected to house the construction workers. *(S. Heyward)*

Farmland, Hatton Road, May 1944. The view is to the east, with Hatton Road and some of the village of Hatton in the distance. *(S. Heyward)*

Devastated farmland, Hatton Road, 1944. The same view just a few weeks later with construction of the airport under way. *(S. Heyward)*

The farm of D. & J. Wild, Cains Lane, Heathrow, 1944. This photograph, looking in an easterly direction, was taken from the bedroom window of David Wild's farmhouse shortly before the farm was requisitioned by the Air Ministry in the summer of 1944. The packing shed and glasshouses were moved to their new farm at Colchester and their value deducted from the compensation the Wilds eventually received, long after the war had ended. *(W. Wild)*

Heathrow Airport looking eastwards from the top of the Queen's Building, 1992. This building occupies roughly the same position as Wild's farm so the two views are comparable. The roof of the Queen's Building was originally open to sightseers but since 2001 it has been closed for fear of terrorist attacks.

Heathrow Hall, 1935. This fine late eighteenth-century farmhouse was the first of the many farmhouses that were dotted along Heathrow Road from the Three Magpies to Perry Oaks. It was demolished in 1944 to make way for the construction of the airport.

Heathrow Hall in the course of demolition, 1944. 'E'en now the devastation has begun,/And half the business of destruction done;/E'en now methinks, as pond'ring here I stand,/I see the rural virtues leave the land', wrote Oliver Goldsmith in his poem 'The Deserted Village'. *(P. Philp)*

Demolition of Heathrow Hall and farm buildings, viewed from the south side of the Hall, 1944. *(P. Philp)*

Further demolitions in connection with the airport development, 1944. Winnie Baker, a land girl, is standing by a partially demolished building in Cain's Lane. It had originally been a Methodist chapel but had been used for other purposes since 1870. In the centre background are four farm cottages, and to their left is Palmer's Farm. *(W. Wild)*

Heathrow under construction, 1946. The Bath Road runs east–west across the lower third of the photograph. South of the Bath Road there is utter devastation but to the north, on the eastern fringe of the photograph, is the village of Sipson still surrounded on all but its southern side by land under intensive cultivation. Sixty years later some of the land is still under cultivation but much has been excavated for gravel. If a third runway were to be built it would run across the top quarter of the picture, and proposals have been put forward for a sixth terminal that would occupy all the land between the runway and the Bath Road. This would lead to the complete obliteration of Sipson and make much of Harmondsworth uninhabitable.

The western end of General Roy's baseline, Heathrow, 1944. The cannon was placed in position to mark the end of the baseline that had been measured across Hounslow Heath in 1784 as part of a trigonometrical survey. The man in charge was Major-General William Roy, 'the father of the Ordnance Survey'. To commemorate the 200th anniversary of his birth a plaque was placed on top of the cannon in 1926. (*S. Heyward*)

Removal of the cannon, 1944. When construction of the airport began the cannon was removed and stored at the headquarters of the Ordnance Survey, then at Chessington. (*M. Heyward*)

In 1968, twenty-two years after its removal, the cannon was returned to Heathrow and stored by the Engineering Department of BAA until 1972, when it was reinstated close to its original position. The photograph shows the cannon in place with the 1926 plaque mounted on a sloping concrete plinth. The plaque records the remarkable accuracy of Roy's measurement of the baseline – 27,404.01 feet by his estimation and 27,406.19 feet as determined by modern methods.

A BOAC Stratocruiser coming in to land in December 1949. The view is to the east from Hatton Road, with the turning into Cains Lane at the extreme left. *(Hounslow Library)*

A 2005 view from approximately the same aspect.

Above: Smallholding, Burrows Hill Close, Heathrow. *Below:* Demolitions in Burrows Hill Close prior to the construction of Terminal 5. After the First World War Middlesex County Council established twenty-four smallholdings to the west of the Perry Oaks sludge works. They consisted of small two-storey houses with steeply pitched roofs and eaves at first-floor level, each with a plot of land attached. They comprised the Burrows Hill Close estate and Bedfont Court estate to the north of Spout Lane and were separated from each other when Stanwell Moor Road was built in 1948. Although in the shadow of the airport, they survived until 2001 when the Burrows Hill estate became part of the Terminal 5 complex and the Bedfont Court estate was excavated for gravel. The photographs show that the terminal was not built only on the site of a sludge works.

2

The Bath Road & Longford

Top: Bath Road, looking west from Cranford Bridge in the early 1900s, with the White Hart on the left and the old Berkeley Arms on the right. The large building to the right of the White Hart was Cranford Hall; it and the old Berkeley Arms were pulled down when the Bath Road was widened in 1928. A replacement for the Berkeley Arms was built about half a mile to the east, and this is now part of the Jarvis Hotel.
Bottom: In 2004 the White Hart is the only indication that the two photographs were taken from the same vantage point. Even this is under threat with proposals for its demolition to make way for yet another airport hotel. The present building replaced an inn of the same name, and the stables of its predecessor still remain attached to the western side of the inn.

William Byrd School, Bath Road, Harlington, 1939. Until 1939 the children of Harlington for the most part attended either the National Schools in the High Street or the Sipson and Heathrow School on the Bath Road at Sipson. With the rapid growth in the population of the district in the 1930s Middlesex County Council built a new school named after William Byrd, the Elizabethan composer who lived in Harlington from 1577 to 1593. The school – a brick building characteristic of Middlesex schools of the time – opened in the autumn term of 1939. (*Uxbridge Library*)

Status Park, Bath Road, Harlington, 2004. In 1970 Hillingdon Council decided to sell the school site for hotel development, hoping to raise enough money to build a new school in less noisy surroundings and provide a large surplus for the council's coffers. Unfortunately the transaction was mishandled and the council was left with the old site on its hands. It did build a new school of the same name in Victoria Lane in 1974, but only at the expense of depriving Harlington of some of its public open space. Nearly twenty years after the initial proposals the council did eventually find a buyer for the site and it is now occupied by an office complex known as Status Park.

Ash Cottage, Harlington Corner, 1968. This large house dated from the mid-nineteenth century. After its demolition in the early 1970s the site stood vacant for several years until the Ibis Hotel was built. A part of the caretaker's house at William Byrd School can just be seen on the extreme right.

Ibis Hotel, 2004. The pine tree on the left is the only clue that both these photographs are of the same place.

Hatton Road, Harlington Corner, early 1900s. At Harlington Corner the High Street crossed the Bath Road and continued as Hatton Road (or Lane) leading to Hatton and East Bedfont. Until it reached Hatton there were very few houses along the road because until the Harlington Enclosure of 1821 the area between Hatton and Harlington was part of Harlington Common.

Hatton Road, 2004. The northern part of Hatton Road was closed in 1944 when construction of the airport began and only the first few hundred yards are now left of the old alignment. The remainder between the Bath Road and the Great South-West Road is now an integral part of the airport. Surprisingly the house on the right has survived from the pre-airport era. It dates from the 1930s and is now used as offices under the name Stoic House.

The Coach and Horses, Harlington Corner, 1931. This old coaching inn was built in about 1769 and needlessly demolished when the hotel shown below was built immediately behind it.

The Heathrow Holiday Inn, Harlington Corner, 2004. When first built this hotel was known as the Ariel, but the name was later changed to the Post House and more recently to the Holiday Inn.

Harlington Hall, Harlington Corner, in 1955, shortly before its demolition. This mid-Victorian house stood on the north-west corner of the crossroads. Its presence is still commemorated by Hall Lane (formerly Mud Lane), which runs along the northern boundary of the site. After demolition the site remained vacant for many years until the office block known as Capital Place was built in the 1970s.

Capital Place, Harlington Corner, 2004. This was built in the 1970s on the site of Harlington Hall.

Bath Road, Harlington. The top photograph, dating from 1965, shows Soviet cosmonaut Yuri Gagarin on his way back to Heathrow after an official visit to Britain. Gagarin had flown into orbit aboard the Soviet spacecraft *Vostok I* on 12 April 1961, thus becoming the first man in space. He orbited the Earth once before returning for a safe landing in the Soviet Union roughly 90 minutes later. The 1961 flight made him an international hero. Ironically he was killed while piloting an aeroplane on a training flight in 1968. In the background are some Victorian terraced cottages typical of many that lined the Bath Road between Sipson Corner and Harlington Corner. The lower photograph shows exactly the same area in 2004. All the houses on the north side of the road facing the airport were demolished between 1960 and 1990 to make way for offices and hotels. *(Top: The late J. Marshall)*

Sipson Road just to the north of the junction with Bath Road, 1986 and 2004. The houses on the right were built about 1930 and the view remained substantially the same for the next fifty-five years. From the early 1980s a massive building development swept away most of the residential homes close to the Bath Road frontage so that offices now line most of the road just to the north of the airport.

The Three Magpies and Bath Road, *c.* 1910, taken from the junction of Sipson Road and the Bath Road looking in a westerly direction. The Three Magpies, which dates from the eighteenth century, stood at the beginning of Heathrow Road, the entrance to which can just be seen on the extreme left. On the right the building with the spire is the Mission Church of St Saviour's; it was a corrugated-iron structure built in 1880 to serve this part of Harmondsworth parish. It was demolished in 1934 and replaced with a brick building further back from the road. This in turn was demolished when the Excelsior Hotel was built in the early 1960s. The church and the hotel can also be seen in the next two pictures.

The Three Magpies and Bath Road, 1993. Only the Three Magpies remains to prove that this photograph was indeed taken from the same vantage point. Even this building has been drastically over-restored but unlike all the old coaching inns on the Bath Road between Cranford and Colnbrook it has, at least, managed to survive.

Bath Road recreation ground, Sipson, 1931. Before it was moved to its present site in Sipson Way, the Harmondsworth War Memorial Recreation Ground was on the north side of the Bath Road opposite the Old Magpies (see next page). In the background is St Saviour's Church. In the early 1960s the Excelsior Hotel (later the Meridian Hotel and now the Park Inn) and the Airport Spur Road were built on the site. The lower picture shows the 2004 view, with the spot where the little boy was standing now occupied by the signpost behind the white car in the middle of the picture.

The Old Magpies, Sipson, 1950. This attractive sixteenth-century inn stood on the south side of the Bath Road about 100 yards to the west of the Three Magpies. It was prematurely demolished in 1951 and its site used as a car park until 1963, when the Airport Spur Road was built through the area. The lower picture shows the scene in 2004. The Concorde is a half-size replica and not an original.

(Sipson and) Heathrow School, Bath Road, mid-1950s.

Heathrow School, Harmondsworth Lane, Sipson, 2005.

The school was established as Heathrow Elementary School by the local school board in 1875 but permanent premises were not available until the school building was opened in 1877. The school was enlarged in 1891 and soon after became known as Sipson and Heathrow School as by far the majority of the pupils came from Sipson. After 1946 it suffered increasingly from the fact that the main runway at Heathrow was no more than 300 yards to the south. The final blow for the old premises on the Bath Road came when the M4/Airport Spur Road was built through its playing field in 1962. Middlesex County Council therefore built a replacement school in Harmondsworth Lane. The children moved to the new school in 1966 and the old school building was demolished shortly after; its site is now used for car parking.

Foundation stone outside Heathrow Primary School. The original stone, which can be seen under the middle window in the top picture on page 32, was removed when the school was demolished and taken to the replacement school in Harmondsworth Lane. It was installed on the new site but not for long as it was damaged beyond repair when a lorry reversed into it. It was then replaced with the new foundation stone, seen above, recording the history of both school sites.

Schoolchildren from Sipson and Heathrow School waiting to cross the Bath Road in the mid-1930s under the guidance of PC Norris from Harlington Police Station. Very few children from the school needed to cross the road but to ensure their safety a policeman was always in attendance before and after school. The terraced row of cottages behind the policeman is Dalton Villas; in the left background a horse-drawn cart is about to enter Sipson Way. Behind it are some of the houses in Blunts Avenue. *(D. Rust)*

The same scene in 2004. This photograph presents a surprising degree of continuity with the past. Dalton Villas survive, as do the houses in Blunts Avenue, but an ugly airport hotel has appeared between Blunts Avenue and the Bath Road.

The junction of Hatch Lane and the Bath Road, 1935 and 2005. The petrol station on the corner belonged to a man named Woodger, and at this time the junction was known as Woodger's Corner. The petrol station has been replaced by the London Hong Kong restaurant, but the buildings on either side remain.

The Peggy Bedford, at the junction of the Bath Road and Colnbrook bypass, shortly before demolition in 1993. This local landmark occupied a prominent position at the road junction for nearly seventy years. It was built in 1930 to coincide with the opening of the bypass and the licence was transferred from the old inn of the same name that stood further along the Old Bath Road. Had it been built further along the bypass it would probably have survived but the owners decided that, because of its prominent position, a petrol station and a drive-in takeaway would be more profitable. The nondescript replacement buildings are shown in the lower photograph, taken in 2005.

The Road Research Laboratory, Colnbrook bypass, *c.* 1940. The laboratory started life in 1930 on the newly opened Colnbrook bypass, as the Ministry of Transport Experimental Station. In 1933 it became the Road Research Laboratory as part of the Department of Scientific and Industrial Research and later opened a sub-station at Langley. As the work expanded the two sites became too small and in 1966 all the work was transferred to a newly built laboratory at Crowthorne in Berkshire. The site remained in government hands and, because of its close proximity to Heathrow, it proved ideally situated for the construction of an immigrant detention centre. This has grown and grown until it now covers all the land previously occupied by the laboratory.

The Harmondsworth Immigration Detention Centre, 2005.

The Duke of Northumberland's river, Colnbrook bypass, 1990. The river now forms the boundary between the Immigration Detention Centre on the right (east side) and British Airways' Head Office (known as Waterside) on the left (west side). However, when this photograph was taken neither had yet been built.

British Airways' Offices (Waterside), Colnbrook bypass, 1999. This controversial development took place on 13 acres of green belt land in the early 1990s. In return for receiving planning permission, BA agreed to purchase 104 acres of Harmondsworth Moor and lay it out as a public park. The moor, most of which was then owned by Hillingdon Council, had become largely derelict as a result of gravel excavations, so its conversion to a public park therefore had some merit. Harmondsworth Moor has since become a park but it would cease to have any amenity value if a third runway were ever to be built. Cynics have claimed that it could well become part of the airport, with Waterside itself well placed to become an airport terminal.

Hunt's Cottage, Bath Road, Longford, 1935. This is the caption on the photograph, although the house is better known as the Quaker Meeting House. It stands on the south side of the Bath Road almost opposite the old Peggy Bedford and on the edge of the airport perimeter. It was used by the Quakers from 1676 until it was sold by them in 1873. Since then it has been used as a private residence. *(WDLHS)*

The former Quaker Meeting House, 2000. The house remains basically unaltered since the photograph above was taken. However, it has been sympathetically restored and would probably be instantly recognised by the seventeenth-century Quakers.

The Peggy Bedford, Longford, *c.* 1920. This coaching inn, formerly the King's Head, derived its name from the lady who was the licensee for more than fifty years until she died in 1859. The old inn closed when the new inn of the same name was opened in 1930 at the junction of the Bath Road and the Colnbrook bypass – see page 36. *(WDLHS)*

The Stables and Phoenix Cottage, Bath Road, Longford, 2005. The old Peggy Bedford and its adjoining buildings were severely damaged by fire in 1934. The Stables incorporated much of what was left, while some of the timbers and bricks from the main building were used to build Phoenix Cottage on the adjoining land.

College Farm, Longford, *c.* 1900. This building dated from the seventeenth century but its name suggests that there may previously have been a building of the same name on the site. The name derived from the fact that between 1391 and 1543 the manor of Harmondsworth belonged to Winchester College. *(W. Wild)*

Nos 502–18 Bath Road, Longford, 2005. These houses were built on the site of College Farm.

The Square, Longford, early 1900s. The area around the White Horse in the centre of the village is known as the Square. Parts of the timber-framed White Horse in the middle of the picture date from the sixteenth century but it has been much altered. Just behind the public house is the eighteenth-century White's Farm and on the right are the mid-nineteenth-century Maywin's Cottages. All of these and most of the other buildings that can be faintly seen in the distance survive. *(WDLHS)*

The Square, Longford, 2005. Superficially the view has scarcely changed in the last hundred years but the airport boundary is now less than 200 yards to the left of the picture.

The Farm, Longford, *c.* 1907. This house dated from about 1830 and was the home of Henry J. Wild of H.J. Wild and Sons, one of several branches of the Wild family who were local farmers. The two little girls – Peggy and Betty – are the daughters of Henry's son William, who lived at Weekly House just out of the picture to the right. *(W. Wild)*

Site of the Farm, 2005. The farmhouse was demolished in the 1960s and replaced with the office buildings seen here. As a listed building the seventeenth-century Weekly House, on the extreme right, could not so readily be demolished so it was refurbished and also converted to office accommodation. Significantly, as with so many speculative office developments around Heathrow, the buildings are now being advertised as available to let.

Looking east from King's Bridge, Longford, early 1900s. The bridge derives its name from the fact that the Crown is responsible for its upkeep. The river which it spans is an artificial channel that was cut in the reign of Charles I to supply water to Hampton Court. The bridge bears the monogram 'WIVR 1834' on each side of both parapets. The houses to the right of centre are Florence Villas and the one nearest the bridge was the village baker's. On the extreme left the roof of the King's Arms public house can just be seen above the bridge parapet. *(WDLHS)*

Looking east from King's Bridge, 2005. The bridge parapets remain unaltered but Florence Villas have been replaced by modern houses. However, the villa nearest the bridge has survived although it is no longer a shop.

Looking west from King's Bridge, Longford, early 1900s.

The view looks much the same a hundred years later in 2005, but it largely fails to reveal the existence of a busy roundabout where Stanwell Moor Road crosses the Old Bath Road. Stanwell Moor Road (then known as Stanwell New Road) was constructed in the late 1940s to replace all the north–south roads that had been closed by the development of Heathrow Airport.

Harmondsworth Fire Brigade, *c.* 1880. The fire engine and firemen are standing in front of the Gable Stores. The driver of the engine is William Hissey. Seated, left to right, are Isaac Blondell (also sexton and gravedigger), W. Belch and D. Nicholls. Standing are H.C. Belch (chief and father of W.), Tom Truss (also village blacksmith) and Samuel Bateman (later to become chief). The fourth man is unknown. At the window is Mrs Sophia Ashby. *(D. Rust)*

The Harmondsworth fire engine, 2003. The fire engine eventually became the property of Hillingdon Council as the legal successor to Harmondsworth Parish Council. Hillingdon lent the engine, in good faith, to the London Fire Brigade to place in its museum. Through an administrative blunder it was put up for sale but fortunately it fell into the safe hands of a local farmer, Mr Roy Barwick. It is now back in Harmondsworth, where Mr Barwick has gone to great trouble to renovate it. From time to time, as here, he displays the engine at local functions.

3

Harmondsworth & Sipson

Funeral of Pte J. Mitchell. The war memorial in the church records that 417 men from the parish served in the forces in the First World War and of them 92 (an appalling 22 per cent) were killed. One of the first was James Mitchell of Sipson, who enrolled in the Royal Fusiliers at Hounslow Barracks on 3 September 1914. He was only just 18 years old and was swept up in the patriotic fervour that persuaded so many young men that they were embarking on a great adventure. He was concerned that the war would be over before he got to the front, but he had not been there for long before he was seriously wounded. He was brought back to England where he died in hospital on 25 May 1915. He was buried with full military honours at Harmondsworth. *(L. Pocklington)*

Ford, Accommodation Lane, late 1890s. The lane originally led from the Bath Road at Longford to Moor Lane in Harmondsworth and vehicular traffic had to cross the River Colne at this ford. The large market van drawn by two horses was being driven by Tom Mullins and came from Sipson Farm. Vans such as this were generally used to take produce to market. (*L. Pocklington*)

Bridge over the River Colne, Tarmac Way, 2005. This photograph was taken from the same vantage point as the one above but much has changed in the last one hundred years. The ford has been replaced by a bridge and trees have grown up on both banks. This part of Accommodation Lane has been unimaginatively renamed Tarmac Way and it is now a busy road.

Loading a market van, late 1890s. This photograph shows the destination of the van in the previous picture, and the large amount of produce being loaded explains why such a large vehicle was being used. The bushel baskets, which were made locally from willows grown along the banks of the rivers, are marked 'T. Wild'. The photograph must therefore date from before or just after Thomas Wild (1848–1932) took Rowland Robbins into partnership in 1898. This photograph, the one opposite and that below, was probably taken by Thomas Wild, who was a keen photographer. *(L. Pocklington)*

Field women, Sipson Farm, late 1890s. The actual location of this photograph cannot be established but it is probably near Sipson, where most of the land belonging to Thomas Wild was located. Much of the harvesting of vegetables was done by women, who went to great lengths to protect themselves from the sun. Scenes such as this could be seen in the fields around Sipson as recently as the 1950s. The person in the straw hat in the background, languidly watching the scene, is probably a member of the photographer's family. *(L. Pocklington)*

Moor Lane looking west, halfway between the village centre and Duke's Bridge, early 1930s. Many of the houses in Moor Lane were of considerable age but all were in poor condition and condemned as unfit for habitation by the local authority, which built new houses behind them. When the new houses were ready the old ones were demolished and the occupants moved into the new accommodation. *(WDLHS)*

Moor Lane, 2005, photographed from a vantage point slightly to the east.

The Great Barn in the early 1900s. The caption on the postcard claims that the barn belonged to a Benedictine monastery but this is not so. From 1069 until 1387 the manor of Harmondsworth did belong to the Benedictine Abbey of St Catherine at Rouen in Normandy, but it was then acquired by William of Wykeham who gave it as an endowment to Winchester College. The barn dates from about 1450 and was built by the college. It is 190 feet in length, 36 feet wide and 36 feet high, and is considered by many to be one of the finest timber-framed medieval barns in England. Consequently it is a Grade I listed building (one of only two in the Borough of Hillingdon) and a Scheduled Ancient Monument; sadly it is currently under threat from the plans to expand the airport. *(K. Pearce)*

The Great Barn in 2004. Until the early 1970s the barn was in use for agricultural purposes as part of Manor Farm. It was then acquired with the farmhouse by a firm of builders who, in return for being granted permission to develop the Manor Farm complex for office accommodation, paid for the restoration of the barn while preserving its setting. The photograph reveals how well this has been done and is a rare example for this book where the later picture looks better than the earlier version.

The south side of Harmondsworth village street, early 1900s. On the extreme right is the village shop (then Ashby's Stores and now Gable Stores), which dates from the mid-nineteenth century. Beyond Summerhouse Lane are some very fine half-timbered Elizabethan cottages that were wantonly demolished in 1937 as part of a slum-clearance scheme. To the left of the cottages was (and is) the Crown public house, which dates from the seventeenth century. Next to the Crown can just be seen the gate pillars of Cambridge House, which was demolished in the late 1950s to make way for the houses in Cambridge Close.

The village street, 2005. Although hidden by trees, most of the buildings seen in the previous photograph survive, with the sad exception of the half-timbered cottages. Unfortunately car parking mars what would otherwise be an attractive village scene and an astonishing survivor of pre-airport days.

The entrance to Harmondsworth via Hatch Lane, 1967. On the left is the Baptist Church dating from the 1880s and in the middle is what was then the Central Garage, which started life as a builder's yard. To the right of the church and almost obscured from view is Acacia House.

The same view in 2005. The Baptist Church remains but the Central Garage has been replaced by an office block, not unattractive in itself but rather out of character with the surrounding buildings. Permission to build this in a Conservation Area was given in the early 1990s. The development has brought little profit to the owners as the offices have been empty ever since they were built.

The junction of Hatch Lane with Holloway Lane and the village street, *c*. 1910. The view is to the west, looking into the heart of the village. On the left is a row of seventeenth-century cottages (see next page), while across Hatch Lane stands the Baptist Church; on the extreme right is what was then the premises of a local builder, H.C. Belch (later Central Garage).

The same view in 2005. All the buildings on the left still stand but the Central Garage has been replaced with the modern office block described on page 53.

Old Cottages, Holloway Lane, 1935 and 2004. These cottages, which adjoin The Lodge in Holloway Lane, date from the seventeenth century. They ceased to be inhabited in the 1940s but astonishingly have survived and are now used as farm buildings. Although it is not apparent from the exterior, they are timber-framed and because of their age they have a Grade II listing. This gives them some protection from demolition and their rehabilitation to residential use would merit investigation. To the left of the cottages in the upper picture is The Lodge, which was built in the early nineteenth century.

The exit from Harmondsworth village, *c.* 1935. On the left is Holloway Lane, leading to West Drayton, and on the right is Harmondsworth Lane, leading to Sipson. The house at the junction dated from the seventeenth century and was demolished in about 1960. On the extreme left is The Close, which was built in the late nineteenth century.

The same view in 2005. The alignment of the road junction was changed in the late 1960s. The house at the junction was built in the late 1950s when the other houses to its left were built in Holloway Lane. The Lodge can just be seen on the extreme right.

Junction of Sipson Road and Harmondsworth Road, West Drayton, *c.* 1900. This is described on the postcard as Batt's Corner but it was also known as Dell Corner. It is slightly outside the area covered by the book and it has been included because it shows the roads leading from West Drayton to Sipson (on the left) and to Harmondsworth (on the right). *(WDLHS)*

The same view in 2005. The area has changed beyond recognition, although the alignment of the two roads remains the same.

Harmondsworth Lane, approaching Sipson from Harmondsworth, 1950. On the left side of the picture in the distance is a row of cottages known as Cedar Cottages (also known as the 16-row), beyond which stands a detached house. These were all demolished in the early 1960s and the entrance to Heathrow School now occupies the site of the house.

Harmondsworth Lane, Sipson, 2005. The bungalow on the right is still standing, as is the barn in the middle distance. On the left is the entrance to Heathrow School.

Sipson Farm, 1969. At the turn of the nineteenth century various branches of the Wild family were farming in the locality, the most successful being Thomas Wild and Son of Sipson Farm. In 1898 Thomas Wild took a junior partner, Rowland Robbins, to form the firm of Wild and Robbins, which became the best known farming enterprise in west Middlesex. It was based at Sipson Farm and the large farm buildings shown here give an indication of its prosperity. The farm survived until the early 1970s and the farm buildings were pulled down to make way for housing about ten years later.

Site of Sipson Farm, 2005. Only the (shortened) brick pillars with their white coping stones, which once marked the entrance to the farm, reveal that this is the same place.

Harvest Supper, Sipson Farm, *c.* 1950. This annual event was arranged by Wild and Robbins and held in one of the farm buildings. All the produce on the farm cart would have been grown locally, mostly on Sipson Farm. At the back on the extreme left is Thomas ('Doughnut') Wild junior and next to him is his father Thomas ('Mazee') Wild. The elderly man in front of 'Mazee' is Jack Andrews. On the extreme right is Linda Mitchell, next to her father Tom, with her grandfather standing in front of them. *(L. Pocklington)*

Preparation of tennis courts and children's playground, *c.* 1910. Messrs Wild and Robbins donated a piece of land in the village for this purpose and the picture shows the preparatory work. In the background are the buildings of Smith's jam factory, the site of which is now occupied by houses in Kenwood Close.

Sipson Tennis Club coach outing, 1936. The photograph was taken at Southend just before the return journey to Sipson. In the 1930s charabanc outings to coastal resorts were commonplace and members of most local organisations would have been given the opportunity to take a day trip by coach to the seaside. For many people, such trips were the only holidays that they had away from home. *(L. Pocklington)*

Entrance to Sipson village from West Drayton, *c.* 1930. In the middle left is the King William public house, the only building that now remains. To its right the prominent building was Centre House, which was then a butcher's shop although earlier it had been the village bakery. On the extreme right is the Welcome coffee tavern and on the extreme left a row of early eighteenth-century cottages. *(K. Pearce)*

The same view in 2005. Only the King William remains; this is a Grade II listed building dating from the sixteenth century. Although disguised by the refronting that occurred in the 1930s it is a rare example in west Middlesex of a Wealden-type medieval hall house. On the left can be seen the brick pillars that marked the entrance to Sipson Farm.

Sipson Gardens, *c.* 1910. This large eighteenth-century house stood at the junction of Harmondsworth Lane and Sipson Road almost opposite the King William. Up to the early 1900s it had been the home of the Appleton family, who owned a good deal of property around Sipson. It was then bought by Charles Ashby and renamed Sipson Gardens. (Prior to this it had had no proper name and was known merely as Appleton's house). In the 1950s it was acquired by a firm of airport caterers and it later became derelict. Although it was a Grade II listed building, no action was taken by Hillingdon Council when, in 1970, the roof and windows were removed. Instead the council later granted permission for its complete demolition, provided that it was replaced by a replica. *(WDLHS)*

Replica of Sipson Gardens, 2005. Superficially it looks something like the building in the photograph above, but it is a complete fake, and does not even stand on the exact site.

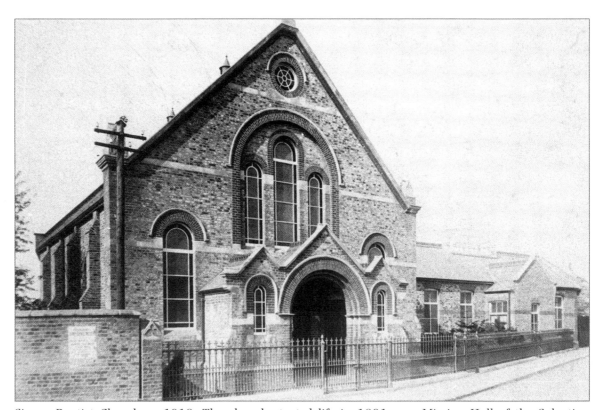

Sipson Baptist Church, *c*. 1910. The church started life in 1891 as a Mission Hall of the Salvation Army, built at the instigation of Thomas Wild. In 1897 it became a Gospel Mission Hall and was enlarged to its present size in 1901. In 1905 the membership of the gospel mission formed themselves into a Baptist Church.

Church Court, Sipson, after its conversion from the Baptist Church in 1988. As the congregation declined, the presence of such a large church in Sipson became difficult to justify, especially as there were large Baptist churches at both Harlington and Harmondsworth. The main part of the building was tastefully converted into flats and the church relocated in what had been the former Sunday School.

Sipson village centre, looking south from the Sipson Lane junction, *c*. 1920. On the left are Appleton's Cottages, which stretched round the corner from Sipson Lane. On the right, partially obscured by trees and its garden wall, is Hollycroft, the home of R.R. Robbins, and in the far distance is Gladstone Terrace.

The same view in 2005. Appleton's Cottages were replaced by shops and modern houses in the 1960s. The oak tree has grown so large that it obscures the new houses in Hollycroft Close that replaced Hollycroft at around the same time. In the middle distance is the Crown public house, which was hidden by the barn in the previous photograph. Gladstone Terrace remains in the far distance.

Sipson village, southern end, looking north, *c.* 1920. Except for the house on the extreme left most of the buildings have survived. On the left are Holly Cottages, built in 1906 and now numbered 432–50 Sipson Road. On the right is Gladstone Terrace, a block of five houses built in the 1880s and now numbered 415–23 Sipson Road. Both sets of houses started life as housing for farm workers employed by Messrs Wild and Robbins of Sipson Farm. In the middle distance is the Crown public house and in the far distance the Baptist Church. *(K. Pearce)*

Sipson village, southern end, 2005.

Leek planting, Sipson Farm, 1950. The planting machine is drawn by a tractor driven by Henry Belcher. On the machine Len Emery is doling out the young leeks to Messrs Summerfield, Cowan and Pert, who placed them between the machine's open jaws on a continuous belt running horizontally in front of them. The jaws then closed and rotated through 90 degrees so that the leeks could be inserted into the soil.

Airport Spur Road and Holiday Inn, 2004. Much of the leek field in the previous picture was buried under concrete when the spur road between Heathrow Airport and the M4 was constructed in the early 1960s. Dominating the scene is the Holiday Inn Hotel, that started life in 1969 as the Post House Hotel and was built despite public opposition. Permission was allowed on the grounds that 'an hotel standing about 120 feet, would do no violence to the M4 or its surroundings'.

Wall Gardens Farm, Sipson Lane, 1968 and 2004. This farm was originally the most elaborate of the many orchards in the area. Some 16 acres in extent, it was surrounded by a high wall. Within this area the orchard was divided into rectangles, each of which was also surrounded by a high wall. The walls helped to protect the trees from cold winds and frost. By 1970 most of the trees had been removed. The farmhouse and the walls still remain but the whole site is now used for off-airport parking, despite the fact that the site is in the green belt.

4

Harlington

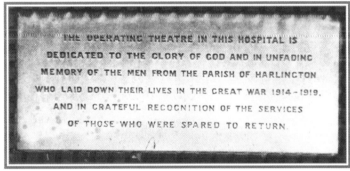

Top: The Harlington, Harmondsworth and Cranford Hospital was opened in Sipson Lane in 1884 as a joint venture of the three parish councils. After the First World War, Harlington Parish Council organised subscriptions to pay for the construction of an operating theatre in memory of the men from Harlington who had been killed in the war. This plaque was placed on the wall of the theatre to record the 'unfading memory' of the war dead.

Bottom: Former Cottage Hospital, Sipson Lane, Harlington, 2000. The hospital closed in 1974 and the building was sold by the Hillingdon Health Authority. It is now owned by the Sant Nirankari Mandal Brotherhood.

Harlington Senior School, New Road, 1929. This school was opened by Middlesex County Council exclusively for pupils from the age of 11 to 14 who had failed to meet the entry requirements of the county grammar schools and technical schools. Similar senior schools were opened throughout the county, thus instituting a system of education that the rest of the country was not to see until the passing of the 1944 Education Act. After this act the school was renamed Harlington Secondary Modern School and it continued under this name until the introduction of comprehensive education in the area. It closed in the early 1990s when the pupils were transferred to the school in Pinkwell Lane (see below). The building was eventually demolished in 1995 and its site used as a car park for the adjacent airport hotel. *(Uxbridge Library)*.

Harlington Community School, Pinkwell Lane. This school was built as a replacement for the school pictured above, but the shed-like structure compares very unfavourably with its red-brick predecessor.

The Pheasant, West End Lane, *c.* 1930. At this time West End was separated from Harlington and regarded as a distinct hamlet. The public house, which is a listed building, dates from the mid-eighteenth century.

The Pheasant, 2005. Although its external appearance is marred by advertisements, the building has changed little in the intervening years. However, what was a country lane in 1930 is now a busy thoroughfare with houses on either side for the whole of its length.

The Elms, High Street, *c.* 1916. This mid-nineteenth-century house was at the time the home of Ebenezer Heyward, the owner of one of the largest farms in the village. It was one of several large houses in the High Street occupied by local farmers, reflecting the agricultural prosperity of the area. It stood on the east side of the High Street immediately opposite the junction with West End Lane. It was demolished in the early 1960s. *(S. Heyward)*

Houses, High Street, 2005. The block of terraced houses on the left were built on the site of The Elms, while those on the right were built on the site of another large house known as Little Elms.

Car sales, High Street, 1970. This attractive early twentieth-century house with its large garden deserved better than to be taken over by a car dealer.

Car parking, 2005. Sadly, the house and the car sales have been replaced by an off-airport parking lot.

Maison Sylvia, High Street, 1942. The hairdresser's shop of this name was acquired by F.W. Hodges in 1938 and the shop has continued in the family ever since. On the extreme right is F.W. Hodges himself; third from the right is his son Ken, with his wife second from the left. *(B. Hodges)*

The Hair Shop, 26 February 2000, on the occasion of the retirement of F.W.'s son Brian (centre). To his left is his son Glen, the current proprietor, and on his right his daughter Gail. *(B. Hodges)*

Wheatsheaf Cottages, High Street, *c.* 1930. The left side of this building had been a public house called the Wheatsheaf not long before, as evidenced by the style of the building and the empty inn sign. When the new Wheatsheaf was built on the opposite side of the road the name of this pub was changed to the Original Wheatsheaf and for a short time it continued to trade as a rival to its neighbour. The building was demolished in the early 1930s and the site was used for many years for off-airport parking under the name Stor-a-Car. *(HHLHS)*

The Wheatsheaf Court flats, High Street, were built on the site of the Original Wheatsheaf in 2004.

Southern end of the High Street, looking south, *c.* 1930. The barn on the left obscures the view of the Original Wheatsheaf, while in the middle distance on the left are Sunnyside Cottages. Across the road is the new Wheatsheaf and to the left is a large building then, as now, containing two shops on the ground floor. *(HHLHS).*

Southern end of the High Street, looking south, 2004. Everything has gone except the large building and the Wheatsheaf.

Harlington pond and village centre, *c.* 1920. At this time the village pond (Butt's Pond) was still an attractive centrepiece to the village. Unfortunately the increasing urbanisation of the area led to a fall in the level of the water table so that the pond held water only during the winter months. Because of this it was filled in during the 1960s, grassed over and planted with trees to become what is apparently the village green. On the extreme left is the old Baptist Church, with Chapel Row to its right, and in the middle of the picture is Manor Farm. *(K. Pearce)*

Harlington village centre, 2005. Although obscured by trees, the old Baptist Church still stands on the left while the pond has been converted into a green. Chapel Row was demolished in the early 1960s and replaced with modern houses standing on exactly the same site. Manor Farm disappeared in the late 1930s to make way for the shops in Manor Parade.

Interior of the barn at Manor Farm, 1970s and 1985. The barn, which dates from the eighteenth century, survived the demolition of the farmhouse. However, by the 1970s it was in a ruinous state although the internal timbers were in good condition. Because the barn was on the list of local buildings of historic interest it had some protection against demolition. The decision was therefore taken to convert the building to office accommodation while retaining the timbers. The lower photograph shows how well this was done.

Poplar House, High Street, 1958. This attractive early nineteenth-century house was demolished in the early 1970s and replaced with a block of flats known as Felbridge Court. On the left of the house a single-story extension can be seen. This was a later addition and served as a grocer's shop until it was demolished. *(HHLHS)*

Felbridge Court, 2004. This large brick box on stilts was built on the site of Poplar House in the 1970s.

Red Lion crossroads, *c.* 1920. This view of the High Street looking north shows the Red Lion on the extreme right and in the middle distance the barn belonging to Woodlands. These survive but all the other buildings have disappeared. The white building on the left is Gothic House, which was converted into one large house from a row of cottages. It was demolished in the early 1960s and replaced with the houses in Gothic Court.

Red Lion crossroads, 2004. The Red Lion survives to provide the link with the previous picture. The buildings in the middle distance can be seen in more detail in the next two photographs.

High Street just north of Sipson Lane, looking north, *c.* 1960. On the extreme left is the village forge. To its right stand a pair of 1930s houses, with Dispensary Cottages beyond. Next is Woodlands (see page 83) and to its left is the Woodlands barn that appears in so many photographs in this book.

The same view in 2005. The 1930s houses and the barn are the only survivors from the picture above.

Harlington and Cranford National School, High Street, 1958. The school, on the east side of the High Street, was opened in 1848 next to the site now used by the Harlington Locomotive Society. It was closed in 1939 and the pupils transferred to the newly opened William Byrd School on the Bath Road. The building was then used for industrial purposes until it was demolished in 1962. *(HHLHS)*

Site of the National School, 2004. After the school was demolished the site remained in the hands of the local authority, which took the opportunity to erect a small sheltered housing development.

Woodlands, High Street, 1961. This former farmhouse dated from the eighteenth century and was needlessly demolished in the early 1960s. Its site is now occupied by 178–82 High Street. The barn to the left survives and now serves as a garage for some of the new houses.

The same site in 2004. The new houses were built much further back and a road runs through the site of Woodlands.

Shackle's house, *c.* 1920. This house had no name other than that of its last occupant, Charles Shackle. It stood on the east side of the High Street opposite the White Hart. The main part, seen here, dated from the mid-nineteenth century and it was demolished in 1960 to make way for the flats in Pembury Court.

Pembury Court, High Street, 2004. This block of flats was built in 1960 in the garden of Shackle's house.

Victoria Lane, looking west from the High Street, *c.* 1930. In the Harlington Enclosure Award of 1821 this was designated as Private Road No. 4. It may well pre-date the Enclosure but was clearly intended to provide access to the newly enclosed fields on either side of the road. By the mid-nineteenth century it had become White Hart Lane and the large garden (now a car park) of the White Hart can be seen on the left. The name was probably changed to commemorate the golden jubilee of Queen Victoria.

Victoria Lane, 2004. Apart from the older nineteenth-century cottages at the end of the lane (just visible in the distance in both photographs), all the houses that now line the road were built in 1956 or 1957.

High Street, looking north from Victoria Lane junction, early 1900s. On the extreme left are Rose Cottages, a semi-detached pair of mid-nineteenth-century cottages. Then comes a house of the same date simply called The Cottage. Beyond is Philp's bakery, the entrance to Philp's Farm and Vine House. In the far distance is the entrance to the churchyard.

The same view in 2005. The old buildings have been replaced by modern houses set much further back from the road.

Bletchmore, High Street, *c.* 1910. Bletchmore was one of the many large houses belonging to local farmers that once lined the High Street; only Lansdowne House now remains. Bletchmore was one of the last such houses to be built, by a member of the Philp family, and it remained in the family's possession until its demolition in 1972. The site of the house and its large garden is now occupied by the houses in Bletchmore Close.

Houses in Bletchmore Close, as seen from the High Street, 2005.

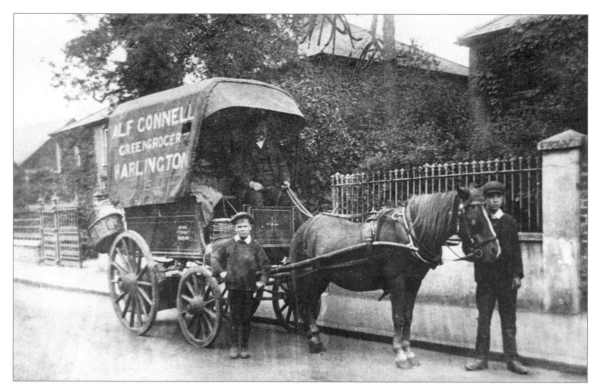

Alf Connell on his deliveries, early 1900s. Alf Connell ran a greengrocer's business from a shop in Chapel Row in the centre of the village. His horse-drawn van is seen here outside Church Villa (on the extreme right), which was then a private school run by Miss Stone. To the left of Church Villa are Lansdowne Villas, two pairs of semi-detached houses belonging to Robert Newman of Lansdowne House.

The same site in 2004. Church Villa was demolished in the 1930s and the site, after staying vacant for many years, became a small housing development in the 1970s. The house nearest the High Street is now the Heathrow Medical Centre. One pair of Lansdowne Villas remains, but the other pair was demolished to make way for modern houses.

Harlington Church from the south-east, 1958. The photograph could have been taken at any time between the restoration of the church in 1880 and the construction of the M4 motorway in 1962. Alas the view is no more, as in 1962 the High Street was diverted across the field in the foreground of the photograph. *(HHLHS)*

Harlington Church from the south-east, 2004. Soon after the diversion of the High Street, planning permission was given on appeal for the construction of a petrol station between the road and the church. The pleasant view of the church from the High Street was thus obscured for ever. The petrol station closed in 1989 and since then the site has had various occupants.

The unveiling of the war memorial, 1921. Seventy-five men from the parish of Harlington were killed in the First World War. A memorial tablet was placed on the wall of the church in 1920 and the memorial cross in the churchyard was unveiled on 18 August 1921. An additional forty-four names were added after the Second World War and one more after the Korean War in 1953. The photograph was taken from the bedroom window of Church Farm and shows the cross being unveiled by the Chaplain General, Bishop Taylor Smith. The other clergyman is the Revd Herbert Wilson, the rector from 1905 to 1929.

Harlington war memorial after refurbishment, 2004.

The Harlington Yew Tree, 1770. The yew that stands to the south of the church porch is now a very insignificant tree but 250 years ago it was the subject of much comment because of the elaborate topiary work that formed part of the annual village fair held at Whitsun. The illustration is a copy of a print published in 1770 by William Cottrell, the parish clerk from 1754 to 1777, with a rhyme by John Saxy, described in the parish registers as a gardener who died in 1741. It is clear from the rhyme that Saxy was responsible for clipping the tree and it is probable that the practice was continued by Cottrell and his son William, who succeeded his father as parish clerk.

The yew tree, 1840, from a drawing by Thomas Scandrett reproduced in *The Literary World* on 6 June 1840. After the death of William Cottrell the younger in 1825 the clipping ceased and, as this print shows, it had almost reverted to its natural shape by 1840.

The yew tree, 2005. Despite suffering repeated damage over the years from gale-force winds, the tree has always managed to recover and, although only a shadow of its former self, it is in a healthy condition.

Harlington Rectory as seen from the churchyard, 1970. Parts of the old rectory dated from the sixteenth century but the main part (shown above) was mostly Victorian. It was demolished soon after this photograph was taken, and most of the trees were cut down to make way for a housing development that did irreparable damage to the peaceful and attractive setting of the ancient parish church.

The same view in 2004. The rectory has gone to make way for a church hall, beyond which, and out of view, are modern houses. Both photographs give a good view of a buttress supporting the wall of the chancel. This and the other buttresses are largely constructed of a ferruginous conglomerate that occurs in the local gravel deposits. The corners have to be made of ashlar stone because of the uneven surface of the conglomerate.

Northern end of High Street, at the junction with Cherry Lane, *c.* 1930. The view is to the north with the beginning of Cherry Lane on the left. On the right is Dawley Manor Farm and to its right, partially obscured by trees, is a large sixteenth-century barn. The old High Street originally continued further north to join Dawley Road and Station Road at the Great Western public house.

The same view in 2004. In 1962 the M4 motorway was cut across the old High Street, turning it into a dead end which was renamed St Peter's Way.

Cherry Lane, *c.* 1930. Cherry Lane led from Harlington to West Drayton, and this photograph shows the beginning of the lane at the Harlington end. On the right is Moat Cottage, built in 1910, which took its name from the moat in an adjoining field that possibly once surrounded Harlington Manor House. On the left are the extensively wooded grounds of Harlington Rectory.

St Paul's Close, 2004. In 1962 the M4 motorway cut Cherry Lane in half and the fragment that adjoined the High Street became a cul-de-sac that was renamed St Paul's Close. Worse was to follow in 1971 when the old Harlington Rectory was demolished and the barrack-like houses seen on the left were built in its grounds. Only Moat Cottage remains, but it no longer enjoys its former sylvan setting.

Dawley Manor Farm from The Moats, 1961. The view is to the east and shows the farmhouse with the High Street running past. The sixteenth-century farmhouse was the oldest and most attractive of the farmhouses that stood in the village High Street. It survived for only eighteen months after this photograph was taken and was the only building in Harlington to be demolished to make way for the construction of the motorway.

M4 motorway looking east, 2004. This now runs across the site of Dawley Manor Farm, which stood in the foreground of this photograph.

Jessop's Pond, early 1900s. This pond was just to the north of Dawley Manor Farm and took its name from a former owner of the farm. Just past the pond on the right is the entrance to Watery Lane and on the other side of the road is The Moats, then a field but now a public recreation ground. It is also known as the Sam Philp recreation ground after the local farmer who donated the land. The pond was filled in during the 1930s after a motorcyclist ran off the road in a fog and was drowned.

The same site in 2004. The site of the pond lies under the M4 motorway but Watery Lane just about survives, although part of it was realigned. Just past the entrance to Watery Lane is Hayes fire station, which was opened on this site in the late 1960s.

Eastfield, Harlington, from the M4 flyover, 1970. The view is to the east with Cranford Park in the distance. Gravel digging began in Harlington in 1967. Up to that time the fertility of the soil had kept the land in agricultural use but from then on the land around Harlington has been released for gravel extraction to such a degree that few virgin fields now remain.

Eastfield from the M4 flyover, 2004. Stringent conditions were imposed on the gravel company to ensure that the land could be returned to agricultural use. This aim has been largely fulfilled although the claim that the land could be restored to its original Grade I agricultural classification has not been met.

Harlington Church from the M4 flyover, 1974. This photograph was taken on the opposite side of the road to the previous two photographs and illustrates that even quite small areas of land have not escaped gravel extraction.

Harlington Church from the M4 flyover, 2004. The gravel workings have been restored and the attractive view of the church for travellers approaching Harlington from Hayes has for the time being been preserved. However, there have been several attempts to build on a site in front of the church, which, if ever successful, would destroy this pleasant vista.

Bedwell Gardens in the late 1920s, with Bedwell House on the right. Bedwell House now looks incongruous and out of place among the modern developments but when it was built it stood in splendid isolation on the south side of the road between Hayes and Harlington. This photograph shows part of the house and gardens which at the time belonged to Herbert Henry Richins. Standing in the greenhouse is his daughter Madge, with his married daughter Nellie Suter on the right. *(A. Richins)*

Bedwell Gardens, 2004. In the mid-1930s the open land surrounding Bedwell House was sold, a wide dual carriageway cul-de-sac leading from Station Road was built and houses constructed on either side. This road was, and still is, named Bedwell Gardens, which was a logical choice of name. In 1963 Station Road was extended southwards to run on an elevated section on top of Bedwell Gardens in order to take it over the M4.

Station Road looking north, *c.* 1910. The view is from just outside Bedwell House and shows some of the late Victorian Villas that started to appear soon after the opening of the nearby Hayes and Harlington station in 1864. Before the station was opened the road was known as Bedwell Lane. This part of Harlington is usually regarded as part of Hayes but the boundary between the two goes as far north as North Hyde Road.

Station Road looking north, 2004. The view is substantially unchanged as all the houses survive but they have lost their iron railings and for the most part their front garden walls. In the earlier photograph most of the front gardens would have glowed with flower beds but now most have been concreted over to allow for car parking.

Dawley Road, looking north from a point just past Redmead Road, *c.* 1930. Dawley Road as far north as Bourne's Bridge is in Harlington, but from there the road forms the boundary between the ancient parishes of Hayes and Harlington.

Dawley Road, 2005. The view is substantially the same, the main difference being in the condition of the road. It now has a good surface with well-defined pavements and none of the horse droppings seen in the previous picture.

5

Hayes

Top: Ford, North Hyde Road, looking west, 1935. It seems incredible that as recently as 1935 traffic was still using a ford. The building on the right was an electricity substation, although judging from the lamppost in the foreground the road appeared to be lit by gas. On the left are some of the houses that started to appear in North Hyde Road in the early 1930s. *(Uxbridge Library)*
Bottom: Bridge over the River Crane, North Hyde Road, 2005. The road was bridged soon after the previous photograph was taken. The absence of traffic shows that this photograph was taken early on a Sunday morning: normally the traffic is so heavy that the bridge is barely visible.

Blyth Road from the railway bridge, *c.* 1910. The houses on the north side of the road date from about 1906 and were built to accommodate workers from the factories being established in the Blyth Road/Clayton Road area. Behind the houses can be seen the first of the multi-storey factory buildings of the Gramophone Company. The factory building to the left of the houses was occupied by the Goss Printing Press Company, an American firm based in Chicago. This building was eventually occupied by EMI (Gramophone Company) until the closure of the EMI factories. *(K. Pearce)*

The same view in 2004. The houses and large factory building remain virtually unchanged but the allotments on the south side of the road were very soon to be occupied by more factory buildings.

Station Road, Botwell, *c.* 1920. The view is to the south, with the junction with Clayton Road at the extreme right. The nearest buildings were known as Glyn Cottages; all had originated as ordinary houses but their front rooms had later been converted into shops. *(HHLHS)*

The same view in 2005. The presence of the large office building on the corner of Clayton Road has changed the scene beyond recognition. But just beyond the corner, and out of the picture, much of Clayton Road has changed very little in the past fifty years.

Station Road, Hayes town centre, 1935. Strictly speaking this is Botwell but even by 1935 it was beginning to be regarded as the town centre. The entrance to Botwell Lane is on the extreme left, while Station Road curves into Coldharbour Lane and East Avenue. The large white building on the right is the Regent cinema. This was demolished in the late 1950s but most of the other buildings seen in the photograph remain. *(Uxbridge Library)*

Hayes town centre, 2005. Following the opening of the Hayes bypass in 1992 the opportunity was taken to close Station Road to through traffic. Otherwise, except for the loss of the Regent cinema, the picture is largely unaltered.

The Ambassador cinema, East Avenue, 1938. This photograph was taken during its opening week in December 1938. The title of the first film to be shown, *This Man is News* (Certificate A), is displayed on the canopy. (*Uxbridge Library*)

BT building, East Avenue, 2005. The cinema was demolished in 1961 and replaced by the BT building. This won a Civic Trust award for design when it opened and the front, as seen here, is not unattractive. However, the large concrete tower at the rear is a good example of 1960s brutalism and is undeniably ugly, particularly when viewed from Hayes town shopping centre.

Botwell Brotherhood Central Hall, Coldharbour Lane, 1981. The Botwell Brotherhood and Sisterhood, both non-sectarian and non-political Christian groups, were founded in 1913. At first the Brotherhood met in a cinema and the Sisterhood in the Baptist Tabernacle Hall, both in Station Road. These sites were then acquired by Woolworths, and the meetings moved to a hall built by the Brotherhood members, also in Station Road next to the post office. In the early 1930s that hall was sold to make way for post office extensions and this hall in Coldharbour Lane was built in 1932. It was demolished in 2002 and replaced with the block of flats known as Brotherhood Court. *(C. Berry)*

Brotherhood Court, Coldharbour Lane, 2004.

St Christopher's School from the Uxbridge Road, *c.* 1960. This large building occupied the corner of the Uxbridge Road and Coldharbour Lane. It was opened in 1901 as the Hayes Certified Industrial School for Jewish Boys. The boys in question were juvenile delinquent Jewish boys and the school was among the first establishments of its kind to train boys for a skilled occupation after release. The school was eventually renamed St Christopher's School and retained that name until it was demolished to make way for the Lombardy Retail Park. *(HHLHS)*

Site of St Christopher's School, 2005. These shops which form part of the Lombardy Retail Park were built on the site of the school. The site is the same but this view is looking west whereas the previous view was to the south, thereby allowing a better indication of the type of buildings that replaced the school. The shops in the picture face Sainsbury's supermarket across a large car park; the Uxbridge Road is to the right with Coldharbour Lane behind the shops.

Botwell House, Botwell Lane, *c.* 1910. This early nineteenth-century house belonged at the time to Edward Nield Shackle, whose family were among the principal landowners in Hayes. He sold it in 1912 to the Claretian Missionaries, a Roman Catholic community recently established in Hayes. They quickly adapted the house for religious purposes and it was gradually extended with the continuing growth of the Catholic community in Hayes. In 1972 a completely new church with a tall bell tower was opened in the grounds of Botwell House. *(K. Pearce)*

Botwell House, 2004. The original house is still immediately recognisable. Part of the new church can be seen on the extreme right.

Botwell Lane, looking north, just south of the junction with Botwell Common Road, early 1900s and 2005. In both pictures the large white house, known as Whitehall, can be seen in the distance. This is the only indication that both views were taken from the same vantage point. (*Top: Uxbridge Library*)

Judge Heath Lane, early 1900s and 2005. The shadows in the earlier photograph suggest that it was taken at midday looking in a westerly direction. The scene has changed so much that it is hard to believe that these photographs were taken from the same vantage point. The lane is named after Judge John Heath, who lived in a large house known as Hayes Park Hall until his death in 1816. He was noted for the severity of his sentences. *(Top: Uxbridge Library)*

The junction of Botwell Lane, looking west along Wood End Green Road, early 1900s. Behind the signpost is the Queen's Head, a small beer house that was demolished in 1939. Just visible above the top of the signpost is London House and on the right, in the middle distance behind the horse and cart, are Mills Cottages. These can also be seen in the pictures on page 114. The entrance to the footpath was just past London House. *(Uxbridge Library)*

The Grange, Botwell Lane/Wood End Green Road, 2005. The old Queen's Head was demolished in 1939 and replaced with the building seen here, which was renamed The Grange in 1986. The white building to the right of the public house in both views is London House.

Wood End Green Road, looking west from a point near London House. Both photographs date from the early 1900s, the lower being a close-up of the entrance via a stile to a footpath leading to Judge Heath Lane. *(Uxbridge Library)*

Wood End Green Road, looking west, 2005. This photograph was taken from the same vantage point as the previous view of the road. It is now completely urbanised and all traces of the pond on the extreme left have disappeared.

Wood End Green Road, looking east, early 1900s. The farmhouse in the picture is Wood End Green Farm, which dated from the eighteenth century. It was demolished in the late 1920s. (*Uxbridge Library*)

Wood End, early 1900s. This area was at the east end of the straggling hamlet of Wood End Green. Grange Cottages are on the left and the Black Horse public house on the right. Church Walk ahead leads to Dr Triplett's School (the roof of which can just be seen). Beyond the school is the churchyard and St Mary's Church. *(HHLHS)*

Wood End, 2005. Wood End Green Road turns the corner to the left at this point to become Queens Road. Church Walk is straight ahead.

Hayes Town Hall (Barra Hall), *c.* 1935. The late eighteenth-century Grove House was bought in 1871 by Robert Reid, who claimed descent from the Reids of the Isle of Barra. He refaced the building in a mock Jacobean-cum-Scottish baronial style and changed the name to Barra Hall. After his death it was sold to a foundation of Anglican nuns and was eventually bought by Hayes Urban District Council to become the town hall. The photograph shows how well maintained were the house and gardens during the 1930s. *(K. Pearce)*

Barra Hall, 2004. Hayes Council ceased to exist in 1965 and responsibility for the building fell to the tender mercies of the London Borough of Hillingdon. As it was no longer the town hall it reverted to its original name but it was sadly neglected and but for the efforts of the local MP it would have been sold to private developers. Thanks to his work the council decided to renovate the building for public use, the renovation taking place in 2005 just after this photograph was taken.

Freeman's Lane, looking east, *c*. 1910. The nearest cottage on the left was no. 18, where Mrs Gibbons committed murder in 1884. It was originally built as a chapel Sunday School by William Hunt, a member of a family firm of local builders. *(HHLHS)*

Freeman's Lane, looking east, 2005. The cottages in the lane were replaced with some council-built developments in the early 1960s. In the distance the house originally known as the Hawthorns (but now the Fountain House Hotel) remains. In the 1930s this house was used as a private school, where George Orwell was a schoolmaster in 1932–3. This fact is recorded by a plaque on the wall of the hotel.

Little Dawley, Church Road, 1961. This house dated from 1787, about the time that most of the much larger Dawley House in Dawley Road was demolished, but the connection between the two, if any, is not clear. At the time of this photograph it was occupied by the Hayes and Harlington Conservative Association. *(HHLHS)*

Hayes and Harlington Conservative Association headquarters, 2005. None of the major political parties has a good record on conservation. The local Conservative Association demolished Little Dawley in 1973, and new offices for the association were then erected on the site of the house.

South end of Hayes village, looking north, early 1900s and 2004. The upper picture shows the original Royal Oak on the left, with the entrance to Freeman's Lane just beyond. In the lower picture the burned-out remains of the Royal Oak are on the extreme left. The original Royal Oak in Church Road dated from about 1840 but it was completely rebuilt in 1937. The replacement building was considerably larger than its predecessor and was built in a mock-Tudor style which fitted very well into the street scene of old Hayes village. It closed as a public house in the late 1990s and fell victim to arson, the site being redeveloped for housing. The large building opposite Wistowe House in the middle distance was the Hayes Town (Congregational) Chapel; this was demolished in 1959 and replaced with a new building which is just out of the picture to the right of the minibus in the foreground. *(Top: HHLHA)*

North end of Hayes village, looking north, early 1900s and 2004. The nearest building on the right is Wistowe House, with Barden House (three storeys) beyond; next is Little Barden House and the projecting front of the shop on the corner of Hemmen Lane. The building on the extreme left was replaced by the present terrace (229–33 Church Road) seen in the lower picture, with the entrance to the brewery (later a laundry) behind; next are four tiny cottages and the Old Crown (the hanging sign of which can just be seen). Round the corner on the left is Church Green. The modern view is recognisably the same, with the addition of the Church Hall on the corner of Hemmen Lane and the early twentieth-century cottages on the left. *(Top: HHLHS)*

Junction of Hayes village street and Hemmen Lane, looking south, *c.* 1900 and 2004. The shop on the corner – once a chandler's, later a butcher's – was replaced by the present Drayton House in 1905. In the middle distance of both photographs are Little Barden, Barden House and Wistowe House.

Church Green, looking west, *c.* 1910 and 2005. The lych gate and the church tower have not changed in the intervening years although the trees have grown to obscure the view of the church. The weatherboarded cottages in the earlier picture dated from the eighteenth century and were demolished in the late 1920s. They were not replaced and the scene is now dominated by parked cars. *(Top: Uxbridge Library)*

Hayes Manor House, Church Road, early 1930s. Despite the name, there is no evidence that a lord of the manor of Hayes was ever in residence. It dated from the seventeenth century but was extensively altered in the 1860s when it became the home of the rector of Hayes. In the 1930s the house was in use as a remand home for boys when the greater part was burned down in a fire. All that remained was the wing on the extreme right. *(HHLHS)*

Hayes Manor House, 2004. The surviving wing of the house is instantly recognisable from the picture above. It is now in the centre of a small housing estate.

The Angel Inn, Uxbridge Road, *c.* 1910. The view is to the east, with Angel Lane just past the inn on the right. An inn of this name, probably the building seen here, is mentioned in the Hayes Enclosure Award of 1814. Unlike the other inns on the Uxbridge Road (such as the White Hart, the Adam and Eve and the Grapes), this one is on the south side of the road. On the other side of the road the entrance to Hayes End Road is just to the left of the horse-drawn cart, with the White Hart largely obscured from view. *(W. Wild)*

The same view in 2005. The Angel was rebuilt in 1926, and every other building seen in the previous photograph has also disappeared. The last to go was the White Hart in 2004 and its replacement, White Hart Court, can be seen under construction on the opposite side of the road.

The Adam and Eve, Uxbridge Road, *c.* 1904. The view is from Church Road, looking north across the Uxbridge Road. This former coaching inn had extensive facilities for coaches and horses in the yard behind. The house to the left of the inn was known as Oakdene, and was the home of Marion Cunningham, a local suffragette. *(Uxbridge Library)*

The same view in 2005. The old inn was replaced with the new building in 1937. Oakdene on the left survives, although it has now been split into two shops.

Yeading Lane, looking north, *c.* 1930. This is probably at the top end of the lane but it is difficult to be sure as the scene has changed beyond all recognition. Until the 1930s Yeading was regarded as the back of beyond, where, according to one chronicler of Hayes, 'Dirt, darkness and ignorance reigned supreme'. This was largely due to the presence of brickfields and their subsequent use for the dumping of rubbish that was brought by canal to Yeading from London. *(HHLHS)*

Yeading Lane, looking north, 2005. The name of the road is the only thing that has remained unchanged. The rural lane has become a busy urban thoroughfare.

Hayes Park, early 1900s. This house, standing alone in very large grounds, dated from the early nineteenth century. Initially a private residence, by 1851 it had become a private lunatic asylum and remained as such until it was acquired by H.J. Heinz Co. Ltd in about 1960. *(Uxbridge Library)*

Hayes Park, 2005. H.J. Heinz Co. Ltd demolished the original house in the early 1960s to make way for the office block seen here. As well as Heinz, the site is now also occupied by Fujitsu Europe Ltd and United Biscuits (UK) Ltd, but the development is in keeping with the area and most of the parkland has been preserved.